THE BRITISH RAILWAYS PILOT SCHEME DIESEL LOCOMOTIVES

Colin Alexander

AMBERLEY

Front cover: It is 10 June 1972 and time has been called on the NBL Type 2 diesel-electric fleet. Equipping them with Paxman engines improved their reliability and extended the lives of those twenty examples, but only by about three years. D6103 heads a long line of her sisters, some green, some blue, at Glasgow's St Rollox works, where they await the cutter's torch. (Keith Holt)

Back cover: A nicely detailed close-up shot of withdrawn No. 24005 at Reddish on 21 October 1976, showing the horizontal bar across the ventilation grille that was missing from most of the later examples. No. 24005 was previously D5000, taking this number because D5005 had been withdrawn in 1969 after fire damage. (Arnie Furniss)

First published 2017

Amberley Publishing
The Hill, Stroud
Gloucestershire, GL5 4EP

www.amberley-books.com

Copyright © Colin Alexander, 2017

The right of Colin Alexander to be identified as the Author of this work has been asserted in accordance with the Copyrights, Designs and Patents Act 1988.

ISBN 978 1 4456 6556 6 (print)
ISBN 978 1 4456 6557 3 (ebook)

British Library Cataloguing in Publication Data.
A catalogue record for this book is available from the British Library.

Typesetting by Amberley Publishing.
Printed in the UK.

Introduction

The British Railways Modernisation Plan of the 1950s featured a scheme to trial small batches of a variety of diesel locomotive types that were designed for different purposes and from a range of manufacturers including its own workshops. This became known as the 'Pilot Scheme', and the idea was to analyse the reliability and performance of these 174 locomotives of fourteen designs in main-line service before placing larger orders.

The Pilot Scheme locomotives were by no means the first diesels on Britain's railways. There had been several experimental examples built as private ventures, such as Armstrong-Whitworth's Sulzer-powered prototype that was trialled on the LNER in the 1930s. There were many diesel shunters in use long before the 1948 nationalisation and, on the main lines, Nos 10000, 10001, 10100, 10201–10203 and 10800 had given valuable experience to the operating authorities. Most strikingly of all, the legendary English Electric/Napier 3,300-hp Deltic prototype of 1955 had turned heads wherever she went. Finally, BR had been using a variety of diesel railcars and multiple units for some time by the late 1950s.

The Pilot Scheme was the first attempt in Britain to order main-line diesel locomotives in quantity, but in a controlled way to allow for long-term evaluation. Unfortunately, in its unseemly haste to eradicate steam traction, BR in its wisdom ordered large quantities of many of these designs before they had been thoroughly tested, which resulted in failures, early withdrawals and even the re-equipping of one large class with new power units at great expense and inconvenience.

Some of the designs, however, were ultimately successful and were perpetuated, lasting in service until the 1990s in some cases. The fourteen classes comprised eleven diesel-electric types and three diesel-hydraulic designs. There were three power categories, Types A, B and C, which later became Types 1, 2 and 4. Type A included freight locomotives of between

800 and 1,000 hp; Type B was for mixed traffic with between 1,000 and 1,250 hp; and Type C denoted heavy-duty locomotives of 2,000 hp upwards.

Three classes were built at BR's own workshops, two at Derby and one at Swindon; four types were built by North British in Glasgow, three by English Electric at Vulcan Foundry, and one each by Metropolitan-Vickers, British Thomson Houston, Brush at Loughborough and the Birmingham Railway Carriage & Wagon Co.

Some of these manufacturers had experience of diesel locomotive production for overseas markets; some had only built diesel shunting locomotives; and others were completely new to the world of internal combustion engines and electrical engineering. The railway itself was not fully prepared for its expensive new toys, and the new diesels had to share facilities with steam locomotives, which was not an ideal environment for such temperamental machines.

The idea for this book came about following the success of a group I started on the website Flickr, which showcases the work of many photographers, and the photographs included are used with their kind permission. They cover the chequered career of the Pilot Scheme Diesels from their birth in the 1950s through wholesale withdrawals beginning in the late 1960s to the present day, showing the fortunate few examples in preservation.

I have tried to select photographs that show each type of locomotive in original condition, as well as covering major modifications and as many livery variations as possible. We will also travel all over the BR network, from the Highlands of Scotland to Cornwall. The book is arranged in order of BR's TOPS classification, starting with Class 15 and ending with Class 44.

In general, the original 174 Pilot Scheme locomotives have not fared well in making it to preservation, with only sixteen survivors, seven of which are Class 26s. By far the most remarkable survivor is Metro-Vick Co-Bo D5705 at Bury, and probably the most unfortunate not to make it into preservation was Baby Deltic D5901, which was scrapped in 1977. Among those preserved is the first of the Pilot Scheme diesels to enter service, D8000 of English Electric Type 1, and she reaches her sixtieth birthday in 2017.

There is a happy ending, however, because royalties from the sale of this book will be divided equally between the group restoring D5705 to working order at Bury, and the group creating the eleventh Baby Deltic D5910 at Barrow Hill.

Co-Bo D5705 had been cosmetically restored and displayed at several open days by 2008, when she was taken into the custodianship of the

Class 15 Preservation Society. They are currently returning sole survivor D8233 to running order, also at Bury. The reason for this partnership was that it was felt that working on two unique locomotives would benefit both machines through their shared knowledge and experience. At first, the dedicated working party spent time sorting out the interior of the Co-Bo, as the engine room and boiler compartment were coated in a thick layer of oily muck. In September 2011 she was lifted from her running gear and both bogies were overhauled. Her five traction motors were then sent away for a full overhaul, despite being found to be in generally good condition. In May 2016 the locomotive was reunited with her bogies and the pipework for the brake system was refitted.

Moving forward, the rewire is ongoing and the B end cab overhaul can commence. The Crossley V8 engine is partially stripped down; this will be completed and then rebuilt using parts from a spare Crossley V12 engine that has been acquired. There is a link to progress reports on the 'Co-Bo' at www.d8233.org.uk/5705.htm.

Meanwhile, when the last-remaining Napier Deltic T9-29 engine, complete with generator and auxiliaries, was bought from the National Railway Museum, not many predicted that it would result in a project to re-create an entire Class 23 Baby Deltic locomotive. At the time of writing this project is approaching the half-way point.

The Baby Deltic Project was established in 2002 to return to operational condition the newly rediscovered power unit. This was in a poor state, although that is no surprise after several years of outside storage. Initial work concentrated on establishing the cause of an engine seizure and determining whether this defect would prevent any realistic opportunity to make the engine run once again. The seizure turned out to be a minor issue and work accelerated to the point where the engine was started in October 2008 for the first time in more than thirty years!

The nine-cylinder Deltic engine was initially mounted in a van before the drastic decision was made to acquire a locomotive, English Electric Type 3 No. 37372, in which to mount the engine for further testing. The 37 contained all the necessary sub-systems, such as radiators, batteries, control gear, etc. With testing complete and the engine running satisfactorily, it was inevitable that thoughts would turn to the potential to recreate an actual Baby Deltic. This potential was realised following the completion of an extensive feasibility study and work commenced on the conversion of the donor loco in 2010. This has involved major surgery to the superstructure of the 37, and the placing of it on a pair of bogies from a Class 20.

The Baby Deltic Project has a website and a Facebook presence, and I would encourage you to take a look at www.thebabydelticproject.co.uk.

Lastly, I must thank all of the Flickr BR Pilot Scheme Diesels group members who contributed their amazing, unique and historic images, and to David Dunn, Sid Sponheimer, Mike Morant, Andrew Lance and finally to Tony at www.rail-online.co.uk for their help. See also individual photograph credits for details.

Thanks also to Adam Booth of the Class 15 Preservation Society and Simon Hartshorne of the Baby Deltic Project for their cooperation; I wish both groups every success with their projects.

Colin Alexander

British Thomson Houston's contract to deliver a class of ten Type A/Type 1 locomotives was fulfilled when D8200–D8209 were delivered to Devons Road depot in East London from November 1957. D8202 stands surrounded by steam-age infrastructure at Norwich on 13 March 1960 in original condition, but with the addition of her running number applied to the nose ends. A Britannia Pacific can be seen on the far left. (www.rail-online.co.uk)

The Pilot Scheme batch of ten BTH Type 1s was constructed by the Yorkshire Engine Co. in Sheffield. They were Bo-Bo diesel-electrics powered by a Paxman 800-hp engine with BTH electrical equipment. They spent most of their lives in and around Liverpool Street, Stratford, Ipswich and Norwich. By the time D8200 was photographed in the early 1960s, she had received small yellow warning panels. (Armstrong Trust)

D8201 is busy with local freight duties at the closed Millwall Junction station in May 1963. The cranes and warehouses of the West India Docks form the background, and there is an ancient grounded wooden coach body in use as a shed. This line now forms part of the Docklands Light Railway alongside the new Billingsgate market. (Tony Powell)

July 1966 is best remembered as the month that England won the World Cup. In the same month and only a few miles from Wembley, D8200 and D8202 double-head a freight train past Stratford. A further batch of thirty-four BTH Type 1s was ordered, this time constructed by Clayton, who were later to be responsible for the infamous Class 17 diesels. (Hugh Llewelyn)

Colchester shed is the location of this fine view of D8203 in January 1968, by which time she had received full yellow ends. This is one Pilot Scheme class that has proven elusive in terms of photographs, although there are plenty of shots around of the later production series. (Bill Wright)

No. 8207 is captured on a rare passenger duty at Woodbridge, between Ipswich and Lowestoft, in the late 1960s. Tolly Cobbold's Station Hotel is now known as The Anchor. All forty-four of the Class 15s were withdrawn between 1968 and March 1971. (Malcolm Dunnett/Armstrong Trust)

Stratford depot was always packed with off-duty freight locomotives on a weekend, and on Sunday 7 June 1970 No. 8207 is parked up with a classmate. I think the 15s suited the small yellow panels better than the full yellow ends. None were painted in BR corporate blue livery despite lasting until the early 1970s. (Gordon Edgar)

No. 8207 is pictured again (note the lack of 'D' prefix), on 2 May 1971, but by now she has been dumped at Ipswich depot, having been withdrawn five weeks earlier. She is accompanied by later classmate No. 8228. Both locomotives would travel to Crewe works for cutting up within a matter of months. (Gordon Edgar)

One solitary Class 15 found itself after withdrawal at the legendary Dai Woodham's scrapyard in Barry, as seen on 5 October 1969. Unlike the many steam locomotives that escaped from there into preservation, however, D8206 was cut up early in 1970. I wonder where those boys are now? (John Wiltshire/Peter Brabham Collection)

Four out of the forty-four Class 15s found further use after withdrawal as carriage-heating units, including Pilot Scheme example D8203, seen here at Finsbury Park on 25 January 1970 as DB968003. Although she was cut up at Colchester in 1981, D8233, one of the other three heating units, would become the sole Class 15 in preservation, and is nearing completion at Bury. (Keith Holt)

The North British Locomotive Co.'s Type A/Type 1 Bo-Bo diesel-electric design, numbered D8400–D8409, was similar in concept to prototype 10800 from the same manufacturer, which was delivered in 1950 to a 1947 LMSR order. Pioneer D8400 is seen passing through York, presumably on her way from the NBL works in Glasgow to Stratford in 1958. (R. F. Payne/Armstrong Trust)

The last two NBL Type 1s to be built, D8408 and D8409, stand inside Doncaster works, where they would be undergoing acceptance trials before delivery to Stratford. They entered service on 25 and 26 September 1958, respectively. The class shared the same Paxman 800-hp engine as the BTH D82xx series above. (Ken Taylor/Armstrong Trust)

The NBL Type 1s were even more camera-shy than their BTH-built cousins as no further orders were placed, meaning that they had a shorter operational life; all ten spent their entire careers allocated to Stratford shed where D8401 is seen *circa* 1961. Note the pale eggshell colour applied to the cab front. A Gresley K3 is visible on the left. (www.rail-online.co.uk)

Looking from the bonnet end, this photograph of D8404 at Stratford in the early 1960s shows that, unlike the front, the rear of the cab was Brunswick Green, the same as the main superstructure. The NBL Type 1s were confined mostly to working East London freight trips for their short working lives. (Armstrong Trust)

There are not many photographs of what would, had they survived long enough, have become TOPS (Total Operations Processing System) Class 16s on passenger duties. This image shows D8400, now with small yellow warning panels, at Liverpool Street station *circa* 1963 on a train including a Gresley coach, probably an empty stock working judging by the disc head-code. (Armstrong Trust)

The other end of D8400 is shown in detail in this 1966 shot of her taken at her home depot of Stratford. As well as local goods trips around East London and Essex, the class could sometimes be found on inter-regional freight workings all around London's suburban lines. (Jonathan Martin)

D8402 is undergoing an overhaul at Doncaster works in this 1960s view, which clearly shows the advantage of 'hood' type diesels over those with enclosed engine compartments when it comes to ease of access for maintenance. (Armstrong Trust)

Last of the class D8409 is sandwiched between a BTH Type 1 and an example of the much more successful English Electric Type 1, D8015, at Stratford in the 1960s. The NBL Type 1s lasted a little over ten years, the first entering service in May 1958 and all being withdrawn by September 1968. (K. Groundwater/Armstrong Trust)

D8408 demonstrates one of Stratford's experiments with different shapes of yellow warning panels. One reason for the rarity of 1960s diesel images like this is that photographers were concentrating on recording the decline of steam on BR. We are grateful, therefore, for the few precious photographic records that were made of these diesel dinosaurs. (Alan Pratt)

D8403, D8402 and D8400 are seen here in April 1969 at Cohen's scrapyard in Kettering, where eight of the ten were scrapped. All were dealt with before the end of 1969. None lasted long enough to receive blue livery, although full yellow ends were applied to many. (George Woods)

D8000–D8019 were the first twenty members of one of the most successful of all the Pilot Scheme classes. This was English Electric's 1,000-hp Bo-Bo Type A/Type 1 diesel-electric, later known as Class 20. Pioneer D8000 stands at Derby Works on 23 June 1958. She had been in service a year. (Unknown photographer, Mick Mobley Collection)

D8003 looks less than clean at Willesden in the company of a sister engine on 18 September 1960. The original batch of twenty EE Type 1s was quickly extended to number 128 examples, their only real drawback being a lack of forward visibility when running 'nose-first'. For this reason, they were often coupled in pairs like this. (N. W. Skinner/Armstrong Trust)

Six years later and also at Willesden, D8001 is seen with small yellow warning panels as she stands under the wires. The Pilot Scheme batch of twenty locomotives were distinguishable from the production series by their oval buffers. Beyond lie examples of AL2 and AL6 electric locomotives. (John Turner)

Unlike the other two Pilot Scheme Type 1 classes, Class 20s received the BR corporate blue livery, and No. 8009 is captured on 11 October 1970 at rest at Toton depot near Nottingham, home to many of the class. The 20s share the distinctive turbocharged whistling sound of their larger relatives, the Class 40s. (R. W. Carroll Collection)

Class 20 locomotives were used over most of the BR network. The former D8002, now renumbered 20002 under the TOPS system, is framed by a magnificent signal gantry near Stirling on 17 June 1983. This photograph illustrates the forward visibility problem, the simple solution to which was to couple them in pairs, with the cabs at the outer ends of the duo. (David Christie)

On 28 July 1984, No. 20050 is in a sorry state at Doncaster works. Formerly D8000, she was the first Pilot Scheme diesel in service, being allocated to Devons Road in June 1957. Happily she is restored to original condition at the National Railway Museum at York. Deltic No. 55016, left, also entered preservation, but No. 40174 beyond was scrapped later that year. (Andrew Cole)

Spending most of their lives on freight workings, each summer the 20s were used in pairs on trains from the Midlands to Skegness, which were favourites with enthusiasts as well as holidaymakers. No. 20013 and production-series loco No. 20047 are at Derby on 13 July 1985 with 1E85, the 09.29 service to the Lincolnshire seaside resort. (Dave Jolly)

Nos 20005 and 20048 head a works train at Nottingham on 4 October 1988. The Clayton Class 17, with its centre cab and low bonnets designed to solve the 20s' visibility problem, was intended to be the 'standard' Type 1 but they were disastrously unreliable and all 117 were withdrawn after a very short life. BR replaced them with another hundred Class 20s from EE in the late 1960s, which brought the total number to 228. (RuntheRedLine)

No. 20008, complete with Kingfisher logo and large numerals, poses among the debris of Thornaby depot with a classmate and a 37 on 1 August 1988. Although the last of the Pilot Scheme examples was withdrawn in July 1993, many of the later examples are still going strong in 2016, giving well over fifty years of service. (Steve Crabtree/Andrew Cole Collection)

No. 20010, photographed at Bescot in Railfreight colours on 31 December 1989, is sandwiched between one of the late-1960s batch, distinguishable by her four-character head-code box, and Class 58 No. 58011, then only five years old. Many of the 228 Class 20s survive in preservation, including three of the twenty Pilot Scheme locos. (Andrew Cole)

This is a rare photograph showing the first two North British Locomotive Company Type 2 diesel-electrics Nos D6100 and D6101 passing Newcastle Central. They are possibly en route from NBL's works at Springburn in Glasgow to their first home, Hornsey in North London, in December 1958. If that is the case they would appear to have travelled via Carlisle. (Ian H. Hodgson/Armstrong Trust)

D6104 is captured on film in the suburban side of King's Cross on 21 September 1959 alongside what appears to be an N2 0-6-2T. The train shed of St Pancras station looms in the background. The locomotives were originally rated at 1,000 hp, later to be uprated to 1,100 hp when the class was expanded to fifty-eight units. (Raymond Embleton/Armstrong Trust)

A trolleybus crosses the bridge carrying Friern Barnet Road over the East Coast Main Line as D6104 leaves New Southgate in 1959, possibly with a Cambridge service; it is made up of ex-LNER Gresley and Thompson coaches and BR Mk I stock. This locomotive was the first of the batch to be withdrawn, in December 1967. (R. G. Warwick/Armstrong Trust)

All of the D61xxs were reallocated to Scotland in 1960, where they would remain until withdrawal. D6102 is parked up at Balornock shed, also known at St Rollox, on 6 September 1962, in the company of first of the production series, D6110. She has been left with her communication doors open; the flexible connection is plain to see. (C. J. B. Sanderson/Armstrong Trust)

Having been transferred to Scotland in 1960 along with her sisters, D6109 is pictured at Stirling shed on 8 April 1963. She has now received small yellow warning panels. The engine room window above the BR emblem would be replaced by additional grilles on the locomotives that were subsequently rebuilt. (C. J. B. Sanderson/Armstrong Trust)

In an effort to improve reliability, twenty of the class had their NBL/MAN engines replaced by 1,350-hp Paxman 'Ventura' engines around 1967. Those that were so treated were given two-tone green livery and, with the exception of D6123, which was first to be converted, they had their disc head-codes replaced by four-character train describers. D6106 is at Stirling, probably with a Glasgow–Aberdeen train *circa* 1967. (R. W. Carroll Collection)

This is a fine colour study of D6101 arriving at Stirling in August 1966. Introduced in December 1958, the last of the class was withdrawn in 1971. Seven of the Pilot Scheme batch of ten were converted to Paxman-engined Class 29s, the un-rebuilt examples being classified 21. (Charlie Cross/Gordon Edgar Collection)

D6109 was unique in that it had the external modifications as per Class 29 conversion, but never received the Paxman engine. As such, it was the only Class 21 to receive blue livery with yellow ends, and four-character head-code boxes. The photograph was taken at Eastfield shed in June 1967; D6109 was withdrawn in April 1968 following collision damage. (R. W. Carroll Collection)

The remaining un-rebuilt Class 21s retained plain green livery and disc head-codes, as seen on D6105, also at Eastfield *circa* 1968, shortly before withdrawal. A rebuilt example is inside the shed, and a BRCW Class 27 is to the left of the shot. All the 21s that were not re-engined were withdrawn by June 1968. (John Turner)

It is 6 January 1969 and you can almost feel the chill as D6102 rests at a snowy Eastfield. She was one of the last to be withdrawn, in October 1971. When the class first moved to the Scottish Region they were initially diagrammed on the three-hour Glasgow–Aberdeen service, but their poor reliability led to them being replaced by Gresley Pacifics. (John Turner)

The 29s were used on the West Highland line from Glasgow to Fort William and Mallaig, and it is there where we see D6101 in September 1969, on a rake of newly repainted blue and grey Mk I stock. Mallaig station has since lost its platform canopy. (Richard Szwejkowski)

Also on the West Highland, blue-liveried D6107 has called at Crianlarich en route for Glasgow about 1969, with a train that includes an ex-LNER Thompson full brake next to the locomotive, and one solitary blue-and-grey Mk I among the maroon examples. The snowy 3,363-foot peak of Beinn Challuim is on the horizon. (M. Halbert Collection/Armstrong Trust)

In contrast to the snowy grandeur of the Highlands, D6107 is captured in the gloom of Glasgow Queen Street station in September 1969. Many years later I travelled in and out of Queen Street on the Edinburgh–Glasgow 'push-pulls' with BRCW Class 27s on each end, and there was always a particularly nasty smell in the tunnels between here and Cowlairs! (David Smith)

A last look at Class 21/29, and the diamond-shaped patch left by the removal of her NBL works-plate is visible as No. 6107 stands between Nos 6103 and 6121 at St Rollox in September 1972. All three would be reduced to scrap within a couple of months, but one of the production series, un-rebuilt D6122, lingered at Barry scrapyard until 1980. (John Law)

In the Flickr BR Pilot Scheme Diesels group that I started online (the contributions to which inspired this book), by far the most elusive class is the North British Type B/Type 2 B-B diesel-hydraulic, of which only six Pilot Scheme examples were built, numbered D6300–D6305. D6300 and D6304 are arriving at St Erth from Penzance on 15 September 1959. (www.rail-online.co.uk)

The Class 22s, as they became, were often used in pairs, and could also be seen piloting steam-hauled expresses. D6304 is seen in tandem with an ex-GWR Hall class 4-6-0 at Aller Junction near Newton Abbot in the late 1950s. The first one, D6300, had entered service in January 1959. (Armstrong Trust)

The Western Region had done its homework on diesel traction and learned from the experience of foreign railways, particularly Deutsche Bundesbahn, where hydraulic transmission had been used very successfully. Another Hall is being assisted by a 22, this time D6301, on what is likely to be a North East to South West service judging by the Gresley stock, as it arrives in Totnes, *circa* 1960. (R. W. Carroll Collection)

The Pilot Scheme batch was employed almost exclusively in Cornwall and Devon. They were powered by the same 1,000-hp NBL/MAN engine as the D6ıxx series, and the power unit was also used in pairs in the larger D600 Warships – more on these later. In this 1962 view, D6300 is working in multiple with D601 *Ark Royal* at Newton Abbot. (Malcolm Foreman/Armstrong Trust)

Even the former GWR's powerful Castle class required assistance over the taxing Devon banks with the heaviest trains. D6305, now with small yellow warning panels, is coupled to one of Collett's four-cylinder masterpieces near Dainton, in Devon, *circa* 1962. Like their diesel-electric Class 21 cousins, the 22s also continued in production to reach a total of fifty-eight units. (R. W. Carroll Collection)

The Western Region led the way in terms of investment in state-of-the-art maintenance facilities for its new diesel fleet. This is Laira depot in Plymouth, where D6305 is seen at rest on 4 June 1962. The Pilot Scheme batch differed in appearance from D6306–D6357, which had a large ventilation grille on the body sides. (Charlie Verrall)

Acquiring four-character head-code boxes that were split either side of the end-communication doors did nothing to improve the aesthetics of these locomotives, and the first version to be fitted looked like an afterthought. D6302 hurries past Plymouth North Road station *circa* 1965, with the ungainly boxes adorning both ends. (Roger Colbeck)

BR's Southern Region penetrated deep into the south-west, thanks to the former London & South Western Railway's 'Withered Arm'. D6302 is seen at the junction station at Bere Alston in Devon, where, until 1966, passengers could change for the Callington branch. That line today is truncated at Gunnislake, and trains from Plymouth must reverse at Bere Alston. (Mike Morant)

D6304 is seen at Penwithers Junction near Truro, *circa* 1967. She has the later, neater version of four-character head-code boxes. This was the junction for the former Newham branch, which was built to give better access to the centre of Truro, compared to the high-level station on the main line. (Sid Sponheimer)

D6300–D6305 were very short-lived, all going by May 1968, and of them D6302 seems to be the only one to be painted rail blue with full yellow ends. D6303 was given an early version of the livery, as seen at Laira on 6 July 1967. Some of the later 22s lasted until early 1972 and D6319 was a preservation candidate until she became the last to be scrapped, in November 1972. (Pete Wilcox)

D6303 and D6305 are seen with production series example D6309 at Laira in June 1967. Notice the spoked wheels. D6300–D6305 spent their whole existence allocated to Laira, although D6300 was based at Swindon for its first few weeks in service, presumably on trials. There is now a 'new-build' project to recreate a Class 22, incorporating an original power unit. (Gordon Edgar)

English Electric made a huge impact with its 1955 prototype Deltic, which subsequently led to an order for twenty-two Type 5s of 3,300-hp. The same manufacturer met the Pilot Scheme Type B/Type 2 brief with a Bo-Bo diesel-electric design that became known as the 'Baby Deltic'. One of these, D5906, enters King's Cross in April 1960 with a mixed rake of stock. (R. W. Carroll Collection)

D5906 again stands at King's Cross, alongside one of the production Type 5s, *circa* 1962. This is D9019 as she was the only one to carry twin air horns on the roof without yellow panels on the nose ends. D5906 has a 1,100-hp, nine-cylinder version of the eighteen-cylinder Napier Deltic power unit that was used in pairs in their big brothers. (Nigel Kendall)

On 20 June 1961, Baby Deltic D5908 makes an interesting comparison with ex-LNER Gresley Class A4 4-6-2 No. 60031 *Golden Plover*, carrying 'The Elizabethan' headboard. Whereas the A4 served her owners for twenty-eight years, the diesel was to last less than a decade. (George Woods)

D5900 entered service at Hornsey in May 1959, after delays due to modifications being made to reduce the weight of the locomotive. The class featured a unique livery style with the red buffer-beam carried around the light green 'skirt'. In this shot taken about 1961, Peppercorn A1 4-6-2 No. 60145 *Saint Mungo* is painted the same dark green as D5900, but you wouldn't think so! (Jack Ray)

The Baby Deltics were not confined to King's Cross and 12 May 1962 sees D5907 in a cutting south of Hitchin with a southbound engineer's train carrying track panels with concrete sleepers. The EE Type 2s were employed mostly on North London suburban services out of King's Cross but were dogged in their early years with poor reliability. (Charlie Verrall)

Following temporary withdrawal, refurbishment and rebuilding, the Baby Deltics' availability improved but no further orders were placed. During refurbishment the Class 23s, as they became, were fitted with four-character head-code boxes and lost the red wraparound paint. In this condition, D5902 is seen at King's Cross in July 1966. (Hugh Llewelyn)

D5906 was photographed at Hadley Wood on 21 October 1966 on a typical Baby Deltic turn, hauling a suburban train made up of the usual Mk I non-corridor stock, one of which is in the new blue livery. Less usual is the inclusion of an ex-GWR 'Fruit D' behind the locomotive. Being a non-standard class of ten, they were all withdrawn by March 1971, despite their improved availability since rebuilding. (George Woods)

On 8 July 1967, English Electric Type 2 D5907 is the subject of this superb study of at King's Cross. These handsome machines clearly belong to the same family, aesthetically, as the more powerful Class 37s and 40s from the same manufacturer. I cannot help but wonder how good those larger locomotives would have looked in two-tone green. (David Quayle)

Like many BR diesel classes, the addition of full yellow ends spoiled the appearance of the Baby Deltics, at least in my opinion. Still in green livery though, with a Brush Type 4 lurking in the background, D5903 is at Peterborough on 7 October 1968. She was withdrawn less than three months later. (Bill Wright)

All but two Baby Deltics were withdrawn during 1968 and 1969, and by 7 June 1970, D5902 was dumped out of use at Stratford, sandwiched between Class 11 shunters Nos 12128 and 12106. D5902 was cut up in August 1970 at Cohen's scrapyard, Kettering. (Gordon Edgar)

Two Class 23s remained in service for another couple of years: D5905 until February 1971, and D5909 hung on until March. The latter was the only Baby Deltic to receive rail blue livery and, on 3 January 1972 they are seen at Stratford, never to work again. Both ended their days at Cohen's of Kettering in August 1973. (John Turner)

They were still at Stratford in April 1972, by which time D5909 had lost a buffer. This is not the end of the Baby Deltic story because, as we will see later, at Barrow Hill in Derbyshire, a group is in the process of recreating a full-size working replica Baby Deltic, to be numbered D5910. (R. W. Carroll Collection)

Although all were withdrawn before they could carry their Class 23 designation, the Railway Technical Centre at Derby retained Baby Deltic D5901 for test trains, but this last survivor still met the cutter's torch at Doncaster as late as 1977. Here she is near Bedford *circa* 1972. (John Law)

D5000–D5019 were BR Derby's Type B/Type 2 Bo-Bo diesel-electric design, with a Sulzer 1,160-hp engine, and they would prove to be a lot more successful than the three Type 2s we have looked at so far. The first few were allocated to Crewe South and Derby, but were quickly loaned to the Southern Region; here is D5003 at Minster in Kent with a local passenger train in late 1959. (R. W. Carroll Collection)

Also in Kent, D5006 stands at New Romney on 26 August 1961. Note the additional SR disc route indicator. The design was perpetuated as Class 24, eventually totalling 151 locomotives, evolving further with an uprated 1,250-hp power unit as the 327 members of Class 25. (Gordon Edgar)

The original batch of BR Sulzer Type 2s was used on the Southern and Midland regions at first but, once the class multiplied in number, they could be seen almost everywhere in Britain, except perhaps the far West of England. D5008 is undergoing an overhaul at Eastleigh works on 31 July 1961. On the right is Ivatt 2MT 2-6-2T No. 41272. (Nigel Kendall)

On 29 March 1965, D5015 is arriving at Bletchley with a stopping train for Euston. She has acquired the obligatory small yellow panel designed to improve visibility for track workers of approaching diesel and electric trains, which were quieter than their steam predecessors. The line to Bedford curves to the right. (Bill Wright)

By 30 July 1966, D5004 is seen under the wires at Bletchley with a freight train. The smaller centre windscreen was to accommodate the end communication doors, a feature that was eradicated in some of the later Class 25s, which also had much tidier bodysides. The new power box replaced the mechanical signal box seen in the previous photograph. (Geoffrey Tribe)

First of the class D5000 had a unique thin white band around her bodywork when new in September 1958. Here she is at Aylesbury with the 14.38 Marylebone–Nottingham Victoria service on 3 September 1966, the last day of through services on the old Great Central main line. (George Woods)

This is a different, melancholy occasion as a pair of Sulzers led by D5009 prepares to leave Olney in Buckinghamshire with a westbound demolition train on 23 March 1967. D5005 sports the two-tone green colour scheme then being applied to new Class 25s. She was an early withdrawal casualty in 1969, as widespread closures led to a surplus of motive power and it was uneconomical to repair her after fire damage. (John Evans)

Another demolition train is at Piddington on 31 March 1967 headed by D5006 in 'economy' green with no lining at all. She is on her way from Northampton to Olney. Her drab plain green livery contrasts with the heavily chromed 1965 Vauxhall Victor 101 Deluxe, belonging to the photographer's father, alongside. (John Evans)

D5011, later No. 24011, is in charge of an ex-LMSR inspection saloon at Crewe on 13 July 1967, and is passing English Electric AL3 class 25-kv electric locomotive E3026 in electric blue livery. Later to become Class 83 No. 83003, she was withdrawn following serious collision damage at Watford in 1975 – the same year that No. 24011 was condemned. (David Quayle)

In the late 1960s full yellow warning panels began to be applied to BR diesels, whether or not the locomotive in question had been painted blue. Also, following the end of steam the 'D' prefix was dropped from the numbers of diesel locos. Both of these changes are in evidence on No. 5004 at Eastfield, in the company of a pair of rebuilt NBL 29s. A steam breakdown crane is rearing its head above. (R. L. Young)

The new order is in evidence at the rebuilt Leeds with freshly repainted No. 5013 in BR blue with new-style numerals. The Class 24 is piloting Sulzer-engined big brother Class 46 No. 153, possibly on the Red Bank–Newcastle parcels train on 30 December 1969. Nos 5013 and 153 would become Nos 24013 and 46016 respectively, under TOPS renumbering in 1973. (John Turner)

In a similar condition to Eastfield's No. 5004, Pilot Scheme Class 24 No. 5012 leads production series No. 5073 as they haul an Up goods train through Crewe on 13 March 1971. Both are in filthy green livery, although the yellow panels have been cleaned. Notice how some of the body-side skirting panels are beginning to disappear. (David Ford)

No. 24010, formerly D5010, is at Doncaster motive power depot on 22 August 1976, having been withdrawn the previous year. The 'blue star' coupling code is prominent, meaning she could work in multiple with the majority of other BR diesel-electrics, with one crew operating both locomotives through electro-pneumatic control. (Trevor Hall)

Another 1976 shot of withdrawn 24s, with No. 24009 and later version No. 24147 at Carstairs shed, the latter taken out of service due to minor collision damage. As you can see, No. 24147 was built without head-code discs and has a roof-mounted, four-character, head-code box like others numbered from D5114 upwards, and in common with the 327 Class 25s. (John Law)

No. 24001, previously D5001, is in an advanced state of destruction at Doncaster works on 18 November 1977. Although none of the Pilot Scheme examples are preserved, having all been withdrawn by July 1976, there are four of the later Class 24s still in existence, including the last to be withdrawn at the end of 1980, No. 24081. (Terry Campbell)

A wonderfully nostalgic view over King's Cross on 20 June 1959, featuring the 'Yorkshire Pullman' stock half-way out of the cavernous station and some early diesels at the stabling point in the foreground. They include two English Electric Type 4s and BRCW Type 2 D5316, then only three months old. Notice the crowd of 'spotters' on the end of the platform. (Ernie Brack)

D5300–D5319 were built by the Birmingham Railway Carriage & Wagon Co. in Smethwick. This Type B/Type 2 Bo-Bo diesel-electric class was initially allocated to Hornsey in North London but migrated to Scotland once a further twenty-seven examples had been added to the first batch. An unidentified example is at Stevenage's old station in the late 1950s. (I. R. J. Woods Collection)

Pictured is another King's Cross view that is full of interest, as D5315 stands at the stabling point *circa* 1959, with a North British Type 2 just visible on the right. A passenger train is arriving behind what appears to be a B1 4-6-0, with Gresley and Thompson stock in both carmine and cream, and the later maroon livery. A pair of Thompson's L1 2-6-4Ts are in the background. (John Law)

Far from the grime of London, the Waverley route ran from Carlisle to Edinburgh through lonely Riccarton Junction. Here we see D5310, now allocated to Haymarket, piloting Gresley V2 2-6-2 No. 60824 on a train of new cars, past Thompson B1 4-6-0 No. 61244 *Strang Steel* in August 1964. When the line closed in 1969, there was widespread dismay at the loss of this iconic route. Amazingly, in 2015 the northern section from Edinburgh to Tweedbank was reopened. (S. C. Crook/Armstrong Trust)

On 6 September 1964 D5310 is seen at the terminus at Silloth, on the last day of services on the branch from Carlisle. The branch utilised part of the old Port Carlisle line, and replaced a canal. Despite being the first line in the country to use DMUs on its passenger services in 1954, it still fell victim to the Beeching Axe. (John Boyes/Armstrong Trust)

Later the same day, D5310 is negotiating a tight curve with a check-rail at Kirkandrews on her way from Silloth to Carlisle. This was the last day of operation on the branch before closure, and indeed this is possibly the last train on this ex-North British Railway line. (John Boyes/Armstrong Trust)

D5316 looks every inch the workhorse as she poses at Carlisle's Kingmoor shed in July 1966. Renumbered 26016 in 1973 she would not carry this identity for long, as she was withdrawn two years later and reduced to scrap in 1976. The forty-seven members of the class shared the same Sulzer 1,160-hp power unit as the D5000s. (Charlie Cross/Gordon Edgar Collection)

D5306 is piloting an unseen Brush Type 4 in a snowy March 1970 under the semaphore signal at Cupar. Just as their Derby-built Class 24 cousins evolved into the more powerful Class 25s, the Class 26 design was perpetuated as a 1,250-hp version, which became the sixty-nine members of Class 27. (Mike Mather)

Now in blue and minus its 'D' prefix, No. 5318 stands at Perth fuelling point on 10 June 1972. Next to her is Brush Type 4 No. 1850, later renumbered as 47200. The Class 26/27 was further developed by BRCW as a bespoke Type 3 for the Southern Region. The six-cylinder Sulzer engine used in the Type 2s was replaced by an eight-cylinder version in what would become the Class 33. (Dave Jolly)

The later version of BR blue livery on Class 26 locomotives featured the yellow paint extended around the side windows. In this condition No. 5308, later No. 26008, is seen at Haymarket depot, Edinburgh, on 12 August 1973. The Pilot Scheme locomotives originally had oval buffers and 'droplight' cab-side windows to distinguish them externally from the later production run. (RuntheRedLine)

No. 26001 is in a severe state of undress as she undergoes an overhaul inside Glasgow's St Rollox works during the open day there on 27 June 1981. I attended this event but my camera was nowhere near as good as this one. I loved the behind-the-scenes feel of such open days, attending similar events at Doncaster, Crewe and Swindon; I can still smell the paint shops! (Russ Watkins)

Looking ex-works as she stands outside Haymarket shed in 1982 is No. 26004, with a Class 25 behind. Many of the Class 26s survived well into the 1990s and seven out of the twenty Pilot Scheme batch are preserved, including No. 26004, which is at the Bo'ness & Kinneil Railway. (Ian Robinson)

This powerful study of No. 26011 under a signal gantry at Inverness, with a Class 20 beyond, was taken on 25 June 1984. In those days the 26s virtually monopolised services on the Kyle of Lochalsh line, but were also used on the route east to Aberdeen and the Highland main line to Perth. She was withdrawn in 1992 and is preserved at Barrow Hill in Derbyshire. (Paul Bettany)

Many of the 26s lasted long enough to receive some of the post-BR liveries, such as No. 26002 here in large-logo Railfreight grey along with an English Electric Class 37 at Eastfield on 25 May 1986. No. 26002 is also preserved at the Strathspey Railway, Aviemore. (Andrew Cole)

The Class 26s were an attractive design, in my opinion, whatever livery they wore; in coal sector 'black diamond' livery, No. 26002 is on the freight-only branch at South Leith hauling loaded 'merry-go-round' hoppers on 25 April 1990. She was one of seven, D5300–D5306, to be fitted with slow speed control specifically for this type of work. (Ernie Brack)

Preserved D5314 is at the Caledonian Railway's Bridge of Dun, together with D5301 on 31 October 2009. Having volunteered on the North Yorkshire Moors Railway as well as for the Deltic Preservation Society, I admire the dedication of those people who give up their time to preserve such machines for posterity. (Anthony Duncan)

Metropolitan-Vickers'Type B/Type 2 diesel-electric Co-Bo design was the most distinctive and possibly least successful of the Pilot Scheme types. With their odd wheel arrangement and 'wonderloaf' profile, D5700–D5719 certainly stood out. D5711 is yet to be adorned with her BR emblem as she passes Melmerby with a test train on the old main line between Ripon and Northallerton in early 1959. (J. W. Hague/Armstrong Trust)

The 'Co-Bos' were built at Bowesfield in Stockton-on-Tees, and each was powered by a Crossley HST-V8 1,200-hp two-stroke engine. They were initially allocated to Derby and employed on the Midland main line, often in pairs on the prestigious 'Condor' overnight Anglo-Scottish containerised freight service. D5705 stands at Derby in April 1959. (Keith Partlow)

On 8 July 1960 the breakdown crew is in attendance, as D5717 has disgraced herself by landing in a turntable well at Derby. The 'Co-Bos' would have become Class 28 but did not survive long enough, and no more were ordered by BR. Having been introduced in July 1958, the last one was withdrawn in September 1968. (Unknown photographer, Mick Mobley Collection)

D5711 is seen at Derby in 1961 with what looks like a rebuilt ex-LMSR Royal Scot to the right. Comparison with the previous views shows how the original wraparound windscreens have been replaced by a simpler design that was not so prone to falling out! D5711 was allocated to Derby at the time and spent a lot of 1961 in the works. (Peter Sedge)

By the time D5702 was photographed at Broughton, north of Preston on a Euston–Barrow-in-Furness train on 26 March 1964, she had, along with her sisters, been banished to Barrow shed. She has also gained small yellow warning panels. At one point in 1960 only three out of the class of twenty were available for service! (R. W. Carroll Collection)

A fantastic shot of D5709 over an inspection pit at Carlisle's Upperby shed in July 1966, with a Brush Type 4 also stabled there. The Metro-Vick carries two shed-codes above the buffer beam. 17A was Derby and 12E was Barrow. The Co-Bos had by 1966 all been reallocated from Barrow to Carlisle. (Charlie Cross/Gordon Edgar Collection)

Another wonderful colour view, this time of D5712 sometime in the 1960s, possibly at Cricklewood. This view from the 'Bo' end of the locomotive shows the smooth side of the body with its cab doors set back a distance from the end. Note also the odd design of bracket for the head-code discs. (Charles Osta)

Compare this view of D5712 from the 'Co' end to the one above, and you can see several ventilation grilles along this side. This is Carnforth shed on 8 October 1966. Carnforth was to become a Mecca for enthusiasts in the early years of preservation, as the shed was reinvented as 'Steamtown', home of *Flying Scotsman* and many other famous locomotives. (John Turner)

It is 1 April 1967 and D5712 approaches Shap station on the West Coast Main Line with empty hoppers to be loaded at the adjacent quarry. The people of Shap lost their passenger service the following year and today's Pendolinos hurtle through the village at 125 mph. The Co-Bos shared the Crossley engine with Metro-Vickers designs for Eire and Australia. (George Woods)

On 26 May 1968, D5712 is in the company of a number of LNER-designed EM1, later Class 76, 1,500-v DC electric locomotives at Reddish, Manchester. She would last another four months in service, whereas the majority of the 76s, which had Metropolitan-Vickers electrical equipment, enjoyed a trouble-free thirty-year career on the famous Woodhead route before their untimely demise. (Gordon Edgar)

Two of the Co-Bos, D5707 and D5708, received full yellow ends on their green livery towards the end of their lives, which did nothing for their appearance. D5707 passes Dallam, near Warrington, being towed to Crewe Works by a Brush Type 4 along with another of the same type. The Metro-Vick lasted in service until September 1968. (Dave Lennon)

Surprisingly, given how early she was scheduled for withdrawal, D5701 went a step further, being the only one to be painted rail blue, representing the new age of British Rail. She is seen at Carnforth in this gem of a picture taken on 25 June 1968, with less than three months remaining before she was silenced forever. (Bill Wright)

At Carlisle Kingmoor on 4 June 1969, D5719 has been stored out of service for nine months, and awaits the cutter's torch. She stands silently along with ten other Co-Bos and thirty-two of the equally unsuccessful Clayton Type 1 Class 17s, one of which is keeping her company here. That is not quite the end of the Co-Bo story, though, as we will see. (John Turner)

After withdrawal in 1968, D5705 went to the Railway Technical Centre at Derby, where she was used on a variety of test trains. Renumbered S15705 she is seen passing East Leake in April 1969. Later, as train heating unit DB968006, she languished in locations such as Swansea, Bristol and Swindon before eventually passing into preservation. She is now at the East Lancashire Railway in Bury. (John Ford)

The remaining Type B/Type 2 diesel-electric design was built by Brush Traction of Loughborough, and differed from the others in having extra non-powered axles to spread their weight, in an A1A-A1A wheel arrangement. D5502 is seen at Stratford on 13 April 1958, only four months after delivery. (Unknown photographer, Mick Mobley Collection)

Two Brush Type 2s led by D5505 pass Tilbury Shed in 1960 with tankers for Shell Haven. Ex-LMSR Jinty 3F 0-6-0T No. 47555 stands at the buffers outside the shed and an ancient clerestory coach stands in a siding. The policeman had just chased the young photographer and his friends out of the shed with a stern warning not to trespass and was making sure they didn't return! (Peter Sedge)

In their early days the Pilot Scheme Brush Type 2s were distinguishable from the later production series by their white cab window surrounds, as seen on D5501 as she passes Forest Gate, running light engine, on 15 September 1963. Brush received further orders, taking the total to 263 units before serious defects were found in the Mirrlees power units. (David Christie)

By 1963, D5513 had lost her white cab surrounds when photographed at Ealing Broadway on an oil train. BR's drastic solution to the Mirrlees engine problem was to re-equip all 263 locomotives with replacement English Electric power units giving 1,470 hp. The unmodified locomotives were designated Class 30, but became better known as Class 31, which refers to the re-engined units. (Nigel Kendall)

The massive water tanks at Stratford dominate this shot of D5503 at her home depot in July 1966. It should be pointed out that most of the trouble encountered with the Mirrlees engines was in the 1,365-hp versions installed in D5520 onwards, so the Pilot Scheme locomotives of 1,250 hp were the last to be fitted with English Electric power units, D5500 being among the very last in March 1969. (John Turner)

D5518 was rebuilt in 1967, after a collision, to the same specification as the production locomotives, and survived as No. 31101 until 1993, thirteen years after the last of her Pilot Scheme sisters had been withdrawn. Here she is with an empty iron ore train in November 1968 at Burton Lane level crossing on the High Dyke branch in Lincolnshire. Her 'blue star' coupling code and four-character head-code box can be seen. (John Ford)

By August 1975 the former D5501 has become No. 31001 under the TOPS renumbering scheme and is in the standard blue livery as she stands at her life-long home shed of Stratford. A weekend visitor to the East London shed in the 1970s would typically be rewarded by the sight of most members of the 31/0 sub-class, as the Pilot Scheme locos had become. (Charles Osta)

Stratford station is the location for this photograph of No. 31003 on 24 May 1979. Most of what can be seen in this image has gone, with the possible exception of the tower blocks, since the area was transformed by the construction of the 2012 Olympics complex and the advent of the Channel Tunnel rail link. (Stuart Ray)

Towards the end of their lives Nos 31005 and 31019 achieved minor celebrity status when they were given red buffer beams and silver roofs for rail-tour duties. The former D5519 is seen on display at Stratford open day on 14 July 1979, where Mr Frosty is doing a roaring trade. Deltic No. 55015 *Tulyar* is visible in the background. (R. L. Young)

No. 31005 is parked outside Colchester depot on 31 August 1979 in the company of a Stratford Brush Type 4 with matching silver roof. Although some of the later Brush Type 2s carried disc head-codes, the majority were built with four-character head-code boxes mounted above the windscreen. One of the former Class 15 heating units is visible behind. (Stuart Ray)

Nos 31015 and 31006 were taken to Doncaster works for scrapping where they were photographed on 27 July 1980. The 'red circle' coupling code denoting their electro-magnetic control gear can be seen above the buffers. Both were reduced to scrap by the end of the year. In contrast, the Class 37 on the left will be overhauled to enjoy many more years of service. (Gordon Edgar)

By 5 October 1980 at the back of Doncaster works, No. 31015 was being stripped down and her English Electric power unit is clearly visible in this view. The fact that some of the production series 31s are still in revenue-earning service in 2016 is ample justification for the inconvenience of replacing 263 Mirrlees engines with more reliable EE units in the 1960s. (Paul Bettany)

Following withdrawal in October 1980, No. 31004 was scrapped at Swindon works in June 1981, but to get from East London to Wiltshire she was taken on a rather circuitous route. She is pictured here looking quite forlorn outside Sheffield's Tinsley depot on 3 May 1981 with a mineral wagon and a snowplough. (Paul Bettany)

Several members of the class found employment as stationary carriage heating units after withdrawal. One such was ADB968014, formerly D5502/31002, seen at Great Yarmouth on 23 August 1982. She was eventually scrapped in 1984. Pioneer D5500 survives in the National Railway Museum at York, wearing her TOPS number 31018. (Gordon Edgar)

Meanwhile, long after her nineteen sisters had turned their last wheel on BR, the former D5518, now No. 31101 is seen at Washwood Heath in a unique livery applied by Bescot depot, on 3 November 1992. Withdrawn two months later, she survives in preservation at the Avon Valley Railway near Bristol. (Andrew Cole)

There was a big gap in output between the most powerful Type B, of 1,250 hp, and the 2,000-plus horse power of the Type C Pilot Scheme diesels, of which there were four classes. English Electric D203 enters London's Liverpool Street station in the late 1950s with a train in a mixture of liveries. A production-series Brush Type 2 and a Thompson B1 complete the scene. (R. W. Carroll Collection)

At Liverpool Street in 1961, ex-Great Eastern Railway J69 Class 0-6-0T No. 68549, dating from 1902, looks immaculate on station pilot duty alongside the new order in the shape of diesel-electric D205. In early 1976 as No. 40005 she was the first of the Pilot Scheme English Electric Type 4s to be withdrawn, along with a few of the later series. (Peter Sedge)

Left: The first of the English Electric Type 4s, D200 was introduced in March 1958. Here she is dwarfed by Liverpool Street's overall roof on 31 August 1963, alongside EE Type 3 D6703, and you can see the family resemblance. Modernisation work is ongoing, as evidenced by the new point motors in the foreground. (David Christie)

Below: D200–D209 were divided between Stratford and Hornsey depots for express services out of Liverpool Street and King's Cross but, by the time the 190 later members of the class were in service, the EE Type 4s were scattered all over the Eastern, North Eastern, Midland and Scottish Regions of BR on all kinds of services. D209 is receiving attention inside Stratford works in July 1967. (Hugh Llewelyn)

A winter's day at Millerhill near Edinburgh in the late 1960s reveals three EE Type 4s, all with full yellow ends. No. 208, still in green but minus 'D' prefix, is nearest the camera. On the left is one of the Scottish Region series 260–266, which lost their end doors and discs in favour of a four-character train describer, but retained the profile above the buffer-beam where the doors had been. (R. L. Young)

In blue livery but retaining her original number, No. 204 is in charge of a train of empty Cartics at Greetland, near Halifax, on 15 June 1972. Note how her marker lights are visible through the opened head-code discs. The Cartic vehicles, articulated in sets of four, revolutionised the transport of new cars on BR, and were in service from 1964 until about 2005. (Terry Campbell)

The Class 40s, as they were known by this time, were often used to haul West Coast Main Line electric services when engineering work necessitated their diversion over non-electrified lines. No. 204 is now renumbered 40004 as she assists No. 86249 at Manchester Piccadilly on 9 October 1977. Her disc-marker lights and cab lighting do their best to bring some warmth to the scene. (Arnie Furniss)

No. 40001, formerly D201, is at Longsight near Manchester, collecting empty coaching stock on 25 October 1977. With their distinctive whistling sound, the Class 40s were becoming increasingly popular with enthusiasts. In the months leading up to this photograph being taken, about fourteen of the class of 200 had been withdrawn. (Arnie Furniss)

No. 40009 was to achieve celebrity status a few years later as the sole remaining vacuum-brake-only Class 40, the others having dual brakes. In 1979 she is seen at Guide Bridge with numerous EM1s, including No. 76009. No. 40009 was eventually withdrawn in November 1984, the last of the Pilot Scheme 40s in service, except for D200 – see below. (Arnie Furniss)

A rare view of No. 40004 with her end communication doors open inside Crewe works in April 1979, alongside Stratford's No. 47130. All but one of the Pilot Scheme Type B and C designs featured these doors to facilitate crew movement between locomotives when working in multiple. In practice they were rarely used and many locos had them plated over. The inner door leading into the cab may be seen. (Charles Osta)

A classic study of No. 40006 as she arrives at York's Platform 15 on 14 June 1980. The Class 40's 1Co-Co1 wheel arrangement was based on that of 10201–10203, the trio of Southern Railway Bulleid-designed diesels, which eventually emerged in 1954. One of these, No. 10203 had the same 2,000-hp English Electric power unit as the 40s. (Gordon Edgar)

A beautiful photograph of No. 40003 hauling a Tinsley–Carlisle goods train past England's highest main line station at Dent on 24 July 1980. This is on the former Midland Railway's legendary Settle–Carlisle line, which by the early 1980s was threatened with closure. Happily, this never happened and the scenery of Ribblehead, Dentdale and Mallerstang can still be enjoyed by rail today. (John Sydney-Han)

No. 40004 is passing Ouston Junction in County Durham with 6S63, the Scunthorpe–Craiginches 'Speedlink' train on 2 September 1982. Next to the East Coast Main Line is Pelaw Grange greyhound track, and the bridge carrying the former Stanhope & Tyne Railway's Tyne Dock–Consett line is in the background, with the connecting spur to the right. (Dave Jolly)

No. 40009 powers through Nuneaton's Abbey Street Junction on 22 July 1984 with 1Z10, the Class Forty Preservation Society's 'Cambrian Coast Express', which ran from Manchester to Aberystwyth and back, via Leeds. Through fundraising on railtours like this, the CFPS was eventually able to secure Nos 40135 and 40145 for preservation, to be joined later by No. 40106. (Russ Watkins)

No. 40004's whistling days are over as she awaits the inevitable at Crewe with three other 40s on 26 January 1986. No. 40009, the last of the original Pilot Scheme batch in service apart from D200, had soldiered on until November 1984, and Class 40 was extinct on BR by early 1985. Nos 40012, 40060, 40118 and 40135 were then given a temporary reprieve in departmental use. (Paul Bettany)

D322 had been withdrawn as early as 1967 following a fatal collision. This meant that, under TOPS renumbering, D200 could become No. 40122. Having been 'mothballed' at Kingmoor in 1982, she reappeared in green livery as D200 as seen at Crewe on 3 September 1987. D200 was finally withdrawn in April 1988 and entered the National Collection. Seven are preserved, but D200 is the only survivor of the Pilot Scheme ten. (Paul Bettany)

D600–D604 were built by North British for the Western Region, and were diesel-hydraulics in the Type C/Type 4 classification. All five were named after Royal Navy Warships. In their early days they were entrusted with the WR's prestige expresses, such as the 'Cornish Riviera Express'. In the late 1950s D604 *Cossack* enters Paddington with the Up service from Penzance. (Alan Curtis)

In 1958 D603 *Conquest* stands alongside one of her four sisters at Penzance. Powered by a pair of the same NBL/MAN high-speed engines as used in the D6100 and D6300 Type 2s, they delivered 2,000 hp. On an early press run D600 demonstrated the advantage of twin engines when one of them cut out and she had to complete the journey using only one. (R. W. Carroll Collection)

D603 *Conquest* stands at Brunel's Paddington *circa* 1959. An ex-GWR 97xx series condensing pannier tank is alongside the new diesel. Apart from brief spells for two of them at Swindon, and one at Landore, the big NBL Warships spent their short lives based at Laira. (R. W. Carroll Collection)

D604 *Cossack* heads the 12.00 Penzance–Liverpool service, which includes a Travelling Post Office vehicle, past Cowley Bridge, Exeter, in 1961. These inter-regional trains to the south west from northern cities such as Newcastle and Liverpool would typically consist of about twelve coaches. On today's equivalent service, passengers are often crowded into four. (R. W. Carroll Collection)

The fuelling point at Old Oak Common depot in West London plays host to D602 *Bulldog* on 27 February 1962. Like the Brush Type 2 diesel-electrics, the D600s utilised the A1A-A1A wheel arrangement, as six axles were needed to spread their weight, but only the two outer axles on each bogie were driven. (Unknown photographer, Mick Mobley Collection)

D600 *Active* looks superb in green with newly applied small yellow warning panels as she is about to leave Plymouth North Road with the Up 'Cornish Riviera Express' on 4 June 1962. No more D600s were built and a combination of reliability issues and their non-standard nature condemned them to an early demise, all being withdrawn by the end of 1967. (Charlie Verrall)

By the time D602 *Bulldog* was pictured at Plymouth in April 1967, she had received an early version of BR blue livery, and her looks had been disfigured by the clumsy addition of head-code boxes on each end. By now the five members of what would have become Class 41 were relegated to mundane duties such as this milk train. (R. W. Carroll Collection)

A unique shot in which the entire class of five NBL Warships is captured, dumped out of use at Laira depot, Plymouth, on 22 April 1968. They had been silenced four months earlier. Nearest the camera is D604, then D601, D602, D603 and D600. They would soon be making their last journey to South Wales. (Keith Holt)

By 12 October 1968 D602 and D603 had been towed to Cashmore's scrapyard in Newport, where they were quickly broken up, a fate that had already befallen D604 at this location the previous month. Here they are amid remnants of some of the steam locomotives they were meant to replace. (Pete Hackney)

D600 *Active* was the first Type C diesel to enter service, in January 1958. She was also the only big NBL Warship to receive full BR blue livery. She was taken to Woodham's scrapyard in Barry in 1968, where she is seen with classmate D601 and Class 21 D6122 in October 1969. The 21 had been withdrawn in 1967 and was apparently used at Hither Green for re-railing exercises. D600 was quietly dismantled in March 1970. (David Goodall)

D601 *Ark Royal* and D6122 meanwhile rotted away in Woodham's scrapyard at Barry for many years and the former was photographed there in July 1970. You can imagine the state she was in ten years later when she was finally broken up in June 1980. When I visited Barry the following month, all I found was a power unit on the ground. (Pete Hackney)

BR Swindon's interpretation of the Type C brief was a unique collaboration with the German builders of the successful DB V200 class, cleverly engineered to fit within the smaller British loading gauge. D801 *Vanguard* is at Paddington in the late 1950s on train 440, the 15.30 Paddington–Penzance, with a Kingswear portion to be detached at Exeter St Davids. (R. W. Carroll Collection)

The D800s were powered by twin Maybach engines giving 2,000 hp and were developed into the production series Class 42 with a higher power output of 2,200 hp, and the similar Class 43, built by North British with NBL/MAN engines. The resultant diesel-hydraulic B-B design was equal in power to, but 55 tons lighter than the EE diesel-electric Type Cs. D802 *Formidable* is at Paddington on 25 August 1960. (Alan Curtis)

D801 *Vanguard* looks rather grimy as she heads a westbound train along the seawall at Dawlish on 23 August 1961. All but two of the eventual total of seventy-one (Classes 42 and 43 combined) were named after Royal Navy ships and so, like the D600 series, they were collectively known as 'Warships'. (Bill Wright)

D800 herself was one of the Warships not named after a naval vessel, being christened *Sir Brian Robertson* after the Chairman of the British Transport Commission. Here she (he?) is in February 1963 with small yellow warning panels in Swindon works between two of the later, larger and more powerful Class 52 C-C Western diesel-hydraulics, whose design was a logical development of the D800s. (Nigel Kendall)

D801 *Vanguard* was captured at Old Oak Common Shed on 14 December 1963. In common with many early diesels, head-code discs had by now been replaced by four-character head-code boxes. D800 had entered service in August 1958, and the other two Pilot Scheme examples followed by the end of the year. Something on the ground appears to be burning. I hope it wasn't the moped. (Fred Steinle/Peter Sedge Collection)

Once the operation of the Waterloo–Exeter service was transferred from the Southern Region to the Western, the Class 42 Warships became a familiar sight on this route. On 10 November 1966 D802 *Formidable* in WR maroon livery is alongside a very grubby Bulleid Pacific at Waterloo. (Ernie Brack)

By August 1967, the maroon paint that was only applied to Warships and Westerns was looking rather shabby on D802 *Formidable* as she approached Salisbury with a Waterloo–Exeter train. The stock includes Mk Is in standard maroon and the new blue-and-grey liveries, together with an ex-SR Bulleid coach in green. (R. W. Carroll Collection)

D800 *Sir Brian Robertson* meanwhile had retained her green livery and, on 23 April 1968, she is seen on a lengthy china-clay train at Fowey in Cornwall. D800 spent her first few weeks at Swindon shed but, apart from that, the original three were Laira engines throughout. The trio were early casualties, being withdrawn between August and October 1968. (Keith Holt)

Maroon D801 *Vanguard* and blue D802 *Formidable* present a sorry sight as they stand outside Swindon works on 5 August 1970. They were both cut up there by November of that year. The production series would follow them into oblivion by 1972, although thankfully, two Class 42s, D821 *Greyhound* and D832 *Onslaught* survive in preservation. (Gordon Edgar)

The remaining Pilot Scheme type comprised D1–D10, which were built by British Railways' workshops at Derby. They were Type C/Type 4 diesel-electrics with 2,300-hp Sulzer engines and were the most powerful of the Pilot Scheme designs. D1 *Scafell Pike* is on show at Marylebone, presumably when new, soon after August 1959. (John Law)

The ten locomotives were named after mountains in England and Wales, hence their nickname, the 'Peaks'. They were initially used on express passenger services on the West Coast Main Line, and D2 *Helvellyn* is at the head of a Blackpool–Euston train passing through Bletchley on 2 December 1961. (Charlie Verrall)

The 'Peaks' shared the 1Co-Co1 wheel arrangement with the D200s, and this excellent colour study of D2 *Helvellyn* at Crewe on 25 June 1964 shows clearly the leading axle with its smaller diameter wheels. Interestingly, in her early days D2 was temporarily up-rated to 2,500 hp for tests on the West Coast Main Line. (David Christie)

D8 *Penyghent* appeared very well looked-after when she was captured during a visit to York on 19 July 1965. The ten Peaks were initially allocated to Camden and Derby, but they all found themselves at Toton depot near Nottingham within a few years. As with many railway locations the willow-herb is growing in profusion in the sidings at York. (Bill Wright)

Looking much grimier than D8 in the previous view, D1 *Scafell Pike* passes Shipley Gate north of Nottingham with a heavy unfitted Up coal train, as a train of empties heads north, in March 1967. She appears to have lost the horizontal stripe on her bodysides. Aside from the eight Warships, the Peaks were the only Pilot Scheme locomotives to carry names. (John Ford)

The Peaks became Class 44, and the design was perpetuated as the more powerful 2,500-hp Classes 45 and 46, totalling a further 183 locomotives. The 44s were then destined to spend the rest of their lives on Midland Region freight services. D1 *Scafell Pike* passes a wintry Kibworth on 22 February 1969 with a long train of mineral wagons. (George Woods)

At Kegworth on the Midland Main Line between Nottingham and Loughborough, D10 *Tryfan* in plain green livery heads an Up freight in March 1969. This locomotive along with D9 *Snowdon* featured a modified design of bodyside grille compared to their eight sisters. (John Ford)

At Normanton on Soar, on the Midland Main Line north of Loughborough, in September 1970, D3 *Skiddaw* passes a milepost as she runs 'light engine' in the Down direction. As No. 44003, she was the first of the ten to be withdrawn, as early as July 1976. (John Ford)

D10 *Tryfan* again, showing clearly the different grille design, passes Toton depot with a train of 20-ton mineral wagons on 6 March 1973. All ten Peaks were built at Derby Works and entered service during a period of six months, beginning August 1959. Under TOPS renumbering they became Nos 44001–44010. (Terry Campbell)

No. 44005 *Cross Fell* is captured in motion as she trundles south with a freight train on the Up slow line at Codnor Park South Sidings, between Chesterfield and Nottingham, on 19 August 1974. At almost 68 feet long and weighing over 130 tons, they were impressive machines. (Les Gregory)

The cooling towers and chimneys of Hams Hall power station dominate the horizon as No. 44010 *Tryfan* heads a train of loaded coal hoppers near Water Orton, between Tamworth and Birmingham, on 26 August 1975. There appears to have been a recent lineside fire. (Russ Watkins)

No. 44009 *Snowdon* had received a replacement Class 45-style nose at one end following collision damage, giving her another distinguishing feature to go with her alternative side grilles. Here she is seen entering Toton yard, with the wagon shops and a Class 08 diesel shunter in the background, on 15 March 1978. (David Hayes)

No. 44010 *Tryfan* was withdrawn in May 1977 and, by the following March, she was standing at her birthplace, Derby works. She has lost her nameplates, some windows and a grille, and is waiting for the cutter's torch, which would come in July of that year. (Charles Osta)

The last three 44s were withdrawn in November 1980, and two are preserved. D4 *Great Gable* is at the Midland Railway Centre, Butterley, and D8 *Penyghent* resides, appropriately, at Peak Rail, Matlock. Here they are reunited alongside another product of Derby works, a 'lightweight' railcar, at Derby Etches Park open day on 13 September 2014. (Stephen Veitch)

Here is the proof that miracle survivor Metro-Vickers Co-Bo D5705 is being restored to working order at the East Lancashire Railway – and your purchase of this book will help safeguard her future. Having been reunited with her freshly overhauled bogies at Bury in May 2016, here we see the battery box being refitted by David Jenkins on 23 July 2016. (Adam Booth)

Your book purchase is also contributing to the Baby Deltic Project, and this shot shows the state of progress in the conversion of No. 37372 to D5910, incorporating an original nine-cylinder Napier Deltic engine and a pair of Class 20 bogies. She is pictured on the turntable at Barrow Hill roundhouse in late 2016. (Simon Hartshorne)